Cult Candy

Where the apparent sweet turns sour

Mike Boyd

KDP

Copyright © [2023] by [Mike Boyd]

All rights reserved.

No portion of this book may be reproduced in any form without written permission from the publisher or author, except as permitted by U.S. copyright law.

Contents

1. To The Disillusioned — 1
2. Does Anyone Understand Me and My Experience? — 7
3. Your Cultic I.D. Card — 13
4. Totalism and Elitism — 27
5. The Sweet — 37
6. Cults Across America and Around the World — 43
7. Groupthink! — 67
8. The Rebuilding Process — 73
9. To The Forgotten Family Members — 80
10. Cults And Law Enforcement — 87

11.	Children Raised from Within	93
12.	Extremity of Doctrine	99
13.	A Ray of Light for The Hurting	105
14.	Everyone Has a Story to Tell	115
15.	Epilogue	129

To The Disillusioned

WHEN A TOXIC PERSON CAN NO LONGER CONTROL YOU, THEY WILL TRY TO CONTROL HOW OTHERS SEE YOU. THIS MISINFORMATION WILL FEEL UNFAIR, BUT I ENCOURAGE YOU TO STAY ABOVE IT, TRUSTING THAT OTHER PEOPLE WILL EVENTUALLY SEE THE TRUTH JUST LIKE YOU HAVE.

At the age of twenty-one, I came to a place in my life where I did a complete one-eighty in the way I lived. I gave up the bottle, the drugs, and the life that was leading me closer to destruction. Although I was a born-again Christian at this point and had been since the age of 17, I had walked a troubled path with little direction, guidance, or boundaries. I was your typical generation "X", latch key kid that was raised in Northern California. When I came to the end of myself, I had recently joined a very conservative church that seemed very attractive and had a lot of boundaries for its congregants to adhere to. This was an attraction to me since I had very few boundaries in my life as I grew up. I thought this was it! This is where I'm going to plant my feet and live a life devoted to Christ. This is where I will ultimately get married, have children, and devote myself to a life of integrity. And; that is exactly what I did! After twenty-four years of being an active participant and having devoted my life to the system and being married to someone who was raised within the church as well as raising our own three children there, I came to a place where I began to question the system, the leaders and my belief system! What I began to see was an abusive totalistic leadership, a pharisaical system that elevated personal preference to doctrinal levels, an elitist mentality among the congregants as well as being within my own heart. Among many other rules and restrictions, we maintained an isolationist stance that kept us from functioning with very few people outside of our circle.

Ultimately, I began to feel that I might be part of a cult. This was a difficult thing to consider since it would mean I had devoted 24 years of my life to a system that was not God-ordained and would put me in danger of retribution from the authority that I was beginning to question. This was a fearful place to be. The questions that came to my mind were many, including: would my wife see what I am seeing, would my three kids see it, am I seeing it correctly, is God helping me to see it, and; is God going to protect me as I begin to impart to others beyond the leadership, our diabolical and at times cruel dysfunction? Yes, he protected me and reassured me over and over that, I would not be touched as I began to project my views. I ultimately believed they were imparted to me by God to project to others that had been a part of the system as well. My wife and my children saw many of the things that the Lord was teaching me that were destructive, too. This was a miracle and helped pave the way to extract all of us from the powerful mental grip that held us.

During the exit process and the years that followed, I began to see the people that I had hurt, the family members that I had little to do with, and the losses that my children as well as my wife had experienced. The pain from these issues troubled, angered, and rocked the core of my soul. I was deeply angered at God and with an unbridled voice, in multiple ways I would express how I felt about it all to Him. When I would look back on those 26 years, I would become perplexed and troubled. It was mentally paralyzing. The newfound freedom that I discovered was becoming snuffed out and I felt like I was alone in a black hole with no one who could understand me and my experience. I was vehemently angry and after 28 years of sobriety, I began to drink again.

TO THE DISILLUSIONED

For those of you who are about to read on and can relate to fellow feelings, I offer you hope and a path to free you from your pain. There is a way out of your deep dark loneliness, anxiety, depression, hatred, distress, the anguish of loss, loss of family and friends, powerful demons that torment your soul, and the hatred you may have residing in your soul toward God. To you, I offer a ray of Light! It is up to you to reach up and out. That is where you must begin. Trusting God or others may be a difficult thing for you to execute at this point in your experience as it was for me at one point. But, I did it! And, I believe in you and that you can do it too. So, read on, and hopefully, you can gain some strength, stability, and insight for yourself. Although this book was written primarily for people who have been impacted by a traumatic religious experience whether directly or indirectly, it has been written for educational purposes as well. And yes, if you are reading purely for entertainment purposes then hopefully you will find something that will help you in your understanding of the religiously abused or oppressed. So, I invite all of you to read on.

Does Anyone Understand Me and My Experience?

GOD ONLY KNOWS WHAT YOU'VE BEEN THROUGH!

In today's world and more specifically America's panoramic view of what a cult is or what it should look like, they often will equate the function to be something similar to The People's Temple and drinking the Kool-Aid (Jim Jones) or David Koresh with his multiple wives and flock of children. He in his last efforts for survival, burned his compound as well as his followers to the ground as the F.B.I.

began their raid of the facility. Or, Warren Jeffs who in the recent past came into the public's eye during prosecution. He was a self-proclaimed profit who had 78 wives and was ultimately prosecuted on multiple accounts of sexual child abuse and placed in prison for a long, long time. The exhaustive list of destructive cults goes on and on.

These types of stories with chaotic endings can cause the former cult member to further isolate after having escaped the powerful grip of a cult. This is not only true for the former cult member but also for people who have been a part of a legalistic or abusive church that has been controlled by a totalistic, narcissistic leader. When former members of a cult or legalistic church want to open up about their experience, they may become constrained by fear of what others may think or how they may respond, or what they might say to others. It can also be difficult for former cult members to explain the unique dynamics or complexity of the cultic structure and function. This fear of sharing their experience is real and they have every right to be protective of themselves, their experiences, and their emotions. The experience that they may want to open up about should only be shared with those who they trust, some therapists, or a self-support group that is composed of people who are willing to open up and share their experiences as well and have their best interest at heart. The support group format will be my focus toward the end of this book.

Other alternatives are available to help a former cult, legalistic church, or abusive religious systems members find mental health help. There are exit counselors who can help process the trauma that was experienced while in a cult or abusive religious organization. Keep in mind, some exit counselors have never experienced being a part of a cult, but they can be of some help. And, when a former cult member decides to become an exit counselor after having worked through their own set of issues that were experienced while in a cult, then they can as well be a source of help and strength to others who are going through the same type of experiences. These types of therapists can be difficult to find.

Some deprogrammers have been used in more extreme cases. This process was or has been typically used when family members hire the deprogrammer to help them with reforming their family members' radical or controversial belief sets or lifestyles. The problem with this process (if the cult member is not willing) is that attempting to make someone see something against their will can be emotionally abusive and possibly implement a form of pressured compliance just like some cults do. Utilizing a deprogrammer requires a willing individual.

Lastly, there are numerous therapists available to help with trauma and assist with breaking down some of the mental confusion, anxiety, and other disturbances that have been experienced during an individual's religious journey. If the therapist has not experienced spiritual abuse, church legalism, or cultic confusion and disturbances, then this may take some time and effort on your part to explain it. In the process of explanation, you will need to, if possible, attempt to be very methodical in revealing your cultic or religious function or experience. It will also require that the therapist truly tries to empathetically understand and doesn't try to remedy too fast or too soon the issues that are presented. This is not ideal but a few of my family members used this process and received some help or benefit. A safe person or therapist will help you become who you are supposed to be. And that is whole!

Your Cultic I.D. Card

Toward the very end of my 26 years of being a part of a cult, I decided to read some books by various authors about cults. Before spending time reading these books, I was beginning to question myself as to whether I might have been an active participating member in one. This was not the first time that I had spent reading books about cults and their function. But this time, I started to read them with the consideration of me being a part of a cult. In times past, I would read about cults but never with self-reflection as to whether I was part of one. This was a scary thing to do. It ultimately shook my world apart once I saw that I was a part of one. It also helped me determine that extracting myself and my family was what ultimately had to happen.

But, before my family's departure, I felt God swaying my heart to share with other church cult members what he had taught me, via a written document. And, that was how the unique dynamics of our church function correlated to me and my family as well as hundreds of people across the country that were a part of the same functioning cult church. When I felt that the Lord was leading me to share these new views, I immediately had doubts as to whether it was the Creator of Heaven and Earth that was swaying me to share it on a national level with the assemblies that were a part of the same functioning cult/abusive church. Some of my immediate thoughts were: I must be crazy, the congregants will think I'm mixed up, I will be pointed out by ministers publicly, my friends and associates would just minimize my credibility, etc., etc.

Before distributing this document that parallels us to the form or structure of a cult and as to whether my fellow brothers and sisters were a part

YOUR CULTIC I.D. CARD

of one too, I wrote three other documents, that exposed our cultic function, that I entitled page 1, page 2, page 3 and page 4 (which was the letter containing the below-stated reasons and questions to help people identify if they were a part of a cult or abusive church). My repeated question to God was, "do you want me to distribute page 4 and will you protect me from the leaders"? He reassured me I wouldn't be touched and that He would protect me. Then the ultimate reassurance that He was moving me to distribute the document came on a cool fall morning. While exiting my vehicle at a place of business that I visited regularly, I looked up from the ground as I neared the building I was heading toward and directly in front of me was a license plate that read "Page 4". At that moment I knew it was God who was moving me to distribute the document that He had inspired me to write.

As you read through the below cultic definers, I would suggest reading through it slowly and thoughtfully considering yourself. I would also suggest reading it more than once. These questions or descriptions are not only for identifying if you are a part of a cult but are also for people to identify if they are part of an abusive church or religious system.

The following are ten ways to Identify if you are a part of an abusive church. 1)control-oriented leadership.2) spiritual elitism.3) manipulation of members.4) a perception of being under persecution.5) a demanding rigid lifestyle.6) emphasis on experience rather than rationality.7) suppression of dissent.8) harsh discipline of members.9) denunciation of other churches.10) a painful exit process.

The following statements are fifty-three reasons to consider if you are in or were in a cult or religiously abusive system

YOUR CULTIC I.D. CARD

1. To think for oneself is suspect in many groups; to think wrongly is satanic.

2. The longer the person was in, the greater the fear of leaving; fear of trying to make it in the outside world, fear of the party's retribution, and fear of nowhere to go.

3. Over time strong willed individuals and independent thinkers became willing participants in a vicious and harmful society.

4. The first condition of milieu control is the limiting of communication with the outside world. The environment is a closed one. As a result, the group became their only reality.

5. All religions have elements of truth. We believe that we have the Greater Truth.

6. Group members believe that the person in power has useful knowledge not available elsewhere.

7. Often the biggest lies are hidden by a compelling context. Later these lies are discovered based on discontinuities that are obvious in hindsight.

8. Because effective manipulators provide as coherent scenarios as possible in which to gain our compliance, detecting discrepant or ulterior motives is difficult.

9. Uncovering oppression or deception for what it is, requires being alert to the role-based constraints of one's own actions.

10. Once aware that their prey is bagged, the slickest operators then emphasize the victim's freedom of choice after tactfully putting constraints on the alternatives.

11. When tightly knit groups are insulated from outside sources of information and expertise and the leader endorses prospective policies before members have a chance to air their views, decision-making processes deteriorate.

12. Do rigid procedural devices limit discussion and suppress unusual suggestions? Any worthwhile association should tolerate dissent, or it should be abandoned.

13. Severing all outside ties for the sake of any social contract increases one's powerlessness within it.

14. The tighter a system is, the more likely minor challenges will be met with retaliation.

15. Legitimate authority deserves respect and sometimes our obedience, but illegitimate authority must always be rejected, disobeyed, and exposed.

16. Basic integrity will usually not allow people to remain a part of a system that victimizes others-no matter how lofty the goals.

17. Cultic friendships usually are conditional, based on the individual's loyalty to the group.

18. Rarely does the initiate understand that he or she will be induced to become involved in a regressive, totalistic environment.

19. Those who attempt to act independently are humiliated by the leader and treated as object lessons for others.

20. The perversion of power that we see in abusive churches disrupts and divides families, fosters an unhealthy dependence of members on the leadership, and creates, ultimately, spiritual confusion in the lives of victims.

21. Manipulative techniques are used to produce conformity.

22. Individuals who join cults rarely know that is what they are doing. They usually believe that they are joining a bible study group.

23. Children raised in cults have little knowledge about the world, especially if their group was isolated.

24. They are socialized into an environment that denigrates independent critical thinking, maintains members in a state of dependency, and fosters private insecurity by attacking members while demanding that they not protest and show a positive front to the world.

25. In most cases, there is one person, typically the founder, at the top of the cult's structure, and decision-making centers in him.

26. Almost all cults claim that their members are "chosen, select, special," while nonmembers are considered lesser beings.

27. Cults are known to dictate what members wear.

28. Cult leaders and con artists are opportunists who read the times and the ever-changing culture and adapt their pitch to what will appeal at a given moment. These manipulators survive because they are chameleon-like.

29. Put forth a closed system of logic and an authoritarian structure that permits no feedback and refuses to be modified except by leadership approval or executive order. If you criticize or complain, the leader or peers allege that you are defective, not the organization.

30. Milieu control also often involves discouraging members from reading anything not approved by the organization.

31. Usually cults do not respect the parental role. Parents are just intermediaries who see that the children obey the will of the leader.

32. Parents in cults are like offspring of the leader and are expected to be his obedient children.

33. A cult is a mirror of what is inside the cult leader. He has no restraints on him.

34. The dreadful belief is instilled by the cult that a person who leaves will find no real life on the outside.

35. In many cases, you no longer have much contact with the outside world.

36. Even though you may not want to admit it, you become completely dependent on the group for all your social needs, your family needs, and your survival.

37. A cult is a world of its own.

38. For people who stay in these organizations, the result is damage not only to their self-esteem but to their whole sense of identity.

39. Members truly believe they will be destroyed if they leave the safety of the group. They think there are no other ways for them to grow spiritually, intellectually, or emotionally.

40. If you control the information someone receives, you restrict his free ability to think for himself.

41. Behavior is often controlled by the requirement that everyone act as a group.

YOUR CULTIC I.D. CARD

42. Guilt is probably the single most important emotional lever for producing conformity and compliance.

43. Information is usually compartmentalized to keep members from knowing the big picture.

44. The doctrine allows no outside group to be recognized as valid, good, godly, or real because that would threaten the cult's monopoly on truth.

45. Problems are always the fault of the member, and due to his weak faith, his lack of understanding, "bad ancestors, "etc.

46. If a cult member raises questions, he is likely to get the "silent treatment."

47. In a destructive cult there is never a legitimate reason for leaving, they are locked in a psychological prison.

48. They believed that they were the only people living as "True Christians".

49. We thought we were The God's soldiers-the only people who understood the bible as it was meant to be studied.

50. Deception includes outright lying, leaving out important information, or distorting information.

51. Another way of evaluating a religious group is the members' freedom to leave. To put it simply, members of destructive cults are psychological prisoners. Destructive cults plant phobias into members' minds so that they fear ever leaving the group.

52. Most cults believe that their group is superior to all other groups and different from all other groups.

53. However, most have to cope with how they treated their family and friends during the time of their cult membership. In some cases, the parent or family member died and the member was not allowed to go to the funeral.[1]

This is a lot of information to ingest and can leave your mind in a quandary. If you find that your religious affiliation relates to many of the above-stated examples, then it is worth considering that you may be part of or have been a part of

---

1. Cults Inside Out-By Rick Alan Ross
    Combating Cult Mind Control-Steve Hasan

an abusive church, religious system, or cult. The greater the number of the 53 examples that apply to you and your experience, then the greater the chance that you are part of or have been a part of a cult. What that number is, I don't know. That is for you to consider for yourself. If you see very few if any that apply to you, then congratulations! But, for the rest of us that it might apply to, then reading on and taking in the rest of the book may be a needed and helpful process as you unravel your own life's experience in a system that may have guided you down a path you would have never chosen. You will experience a lot of emotions. I had a lot of anger when I saw who I was, and how I treated or viewed others and in time became extremely angry toward God. I was also extremely angry toward the leaders of the cult as I reflected on the numerous people I saw verbally abused in public settings.

Ultimately, I was able to laugh a little at the anomalies of our cultic function and behavior. Also, after about four years of absolute unbridled anger toward God, I was able to make peace with myself in my soul and with Him. This happened when I finally came to the place where I realized that God doesn't promise nice and neatly packaged conventional lives to Christians. I thought this was owed to me. Once I saw this then I was able to surrender my anger. This came about during the recovery process that I participated in called C.R. (Celebrate Recovery).

During this program, I was attending and doing some soul searching as relates to my life's drivers, I had an epiphany. And as I read the Bible, I started to realize that most people whose lives were put on public display from Genesis to Revelation, had anything but a conventional life. It was anything but that.

So, my hope for you, my friend, is that you read on. You can be the one who spreads a wake of hope for others who have had similar experiences. There is no personality profile for people who become a part of a cult. So, don't give up! People need you. Yes, I said you.

Totalism and Elitism

PRIDE COMES BEFORE A FALL

Some of you may remember as a child reading one of the most impacting childhood authors of all time, DR. Seuss. Most if not all of his stories would present some type of ethical, moral boundary, or unethical quandary that would stir its readers to see the need to change the conduct of its characters to have a greater outcome for their lives. The story of Yertle the Turtle (published way back in 1958) depicts one of Dr. Seuss's greatest works. If there was ever a book that could shake the core of an adult's soul while reading it to their child, this book is it. It displays the height of pride.

The basics of the story revolve around Yertle the Turtle, the king of the pond (located on the faraway island of Sala-ma-sond), where all of the turtles swim happily. Dissatisfied with the stone that serves as his throne, Yertle commands the other turtles to stack themselves beneath him so that he can see farther and expand his kingdom, each time marveling at what he believes he now rules (like a cow, a mule, and a house). However, the stacked turtles are in pain. A turtle named Mack, who has a checkerboard-style shell and is at the bottom of the pile, is bearing the brunt of the suffering. Mack asks Yertle for a rest, but Yertle just tells him to be quiet. Then Yertle decides to further expand his kingdom and commands more and more turtles to add to his throne. Mack makes a second request for a rest because the increased weight is now causing extreme pain and hunger to the turtles at the bottom of the pile. Again, Yertle yells at Mack to be quiet. Then Yertle notices the Moon rising above him as the night approaches. Furious that something dares to be higher than Yertle the King, he decides to call for even more turtles in an attempt to rise above it.

However, before he can give the command, Mack decides he has had enough. He burps, which shakes up Yertle's throne, and tosses the turtle king off the turtle stack and into the water, leaving him "King of the Mud" and allowing the others to once again swim free, as turtles, and maybe all creatures should.

This story by itself summarizes totalism and a leader reflecting elitism. It's a story that my mother read to me as a child and I'm grateful she did read it to me along with many other great Dr. Seuss stories. But this one impacted me the most. From time to time, I would reflect on it as an adult and in time would read it to my children as they grew up. Sad to say, at times I have acted with the pride of Yertle as well as his inconsiderate heart and have hurt others as a result. This is another, rather large horse pill to swallow, but it is true.

So, you might be asking, what exactly are elitists and what exactly is totalism? I will first define it and then parallel it to my own experience of being a part of a Pharisaical cult church.

Elitists: a select group of people believing they have a special or intrinsic quality that others don't.

Totalistic: a religious or political concept that its citizens or its congregants should be totally or absolutely subject to the leaders' autocratic wills.

Disgusted? Me too! And, when I saw that I had fostered an elitist mentality in my heart, then I became angry at myself and angry about the system that I had been a part of for years. But, how did I get there? How do churches get there? How do congregants get there? Let me explain. When someone's religious upbringing or training or how about we call it "indoctrination" is highly characterized by minimizing the credibility of most other churches or other functioning organizations, and if there is any trust or respect for the leader or leaders who teach these things, then the congregant may begin to develop a sense of "we are the right ones". If the mentality translates to, "we are the right ones", in the minds of the congregants then it can translate into individuals' minds to think, "we must be God's true representation of what His church should look like". At times, some who would minister in the church cult that I was a part of would imply or state as a rhetorical question,"

TOTALISM AND ELITISM

where are the others who want to serve the Lord"? Implying that we were the ones who were truly serving God the right and proper way. This is not to say that I saw other churches as not having Godly, born-again believers but under the surface in my heart as well as others in the cult I functioned in, believed their (outside churches) walk was missing some elements of the standards we adhered to. And, this mentality was not unique to the church I was a part of. And, this does not automatically qualify any church that has this mentality as a cult. But it is a very proud mentality to have as a Christian. It presumes that others' spiritual temperature is lacking and yours is more in favor of God.

On to totalism. Yes, this is another repulsive subject. Although, with this one, I don't need to own very much. Although, I do own that I was very subject or attentive to the leaders as they ministered. I was also very compliant. So, you ask, why would anyone who is part of a church congregation submit their will or walk to the pressured compliance of a totalistic leader? The first thing may be that they believe that they are doing the right thing before the eyes of God. So, they may see it as being done with a willing heart and not considering whether it is manipulative pressure or pressured compliance. They may also be very compliant to avoid public humiliation or punishment. Again, they may have developed a respect or appreciation for the leader or minister that can blur the reality of the totalism taking place in their midst. They may see it as; if this is God's minister and to not comply with his will (meaning the minister) is to be resistant to God. The minister may go as far as saying or preaching, "that to resist the authority is to resist God ". And, this is because God ordained him to be a minister. This creates some other issues. The first is that pressuring compliance with the minister's views of how an individual should walk through their spiritual journey, leaves a gaping hole for an individual to lean on and learn from the Holy Spirit based on an individual's convictions and commitments. The second issue that it creates is that it subtlety implies that the leader is infallible.

In my experience, there were two passages of scripture that were used regularly to manipulate

TOTALISM AND ELITISM

compliance. The first is Mathew 7:16. It states, "by their fruits you shall know them". This was written in the context of identifying false prophets. But, at times in my cultic experience, at the end of a sermon, it was a passage of scripture that was quite often quoted and used in a way to imply that those who do not walk according to his understanding (meaning the ministers) of application of the scriptures or his personal preferences was, therefore, one who was bearing bad fruit. So, as a result, most congregants were compliant. I mean, who would want to be viewed as a bad fruit-bearing Christian? The second is Hebrews 3:17. It states, "have confidence in or obey those who are your leaders and submit to them because their work is to watch over your souls. Sounds pretty clear and very totalistic in a nice way. So, here is some food for thought. But before this, I would like you all to know that I am not a Greek theologian. Let's start with the word submit as used in the passage above. In Strong's concordance (for those of you who may not know what Strong's concordance is, it is a Greek lexicon or dictionary used for bible study) it is stated to mean, give consideration to. "Obey " in this passage means to carry out or fulfill. When you recognize authority, you need to see them as one who is an individual who has information to help guide you. Authority is not to be the one that controls your walk-through pressure and manipulation. I would simply state when it is written in black and white in the scripture and isn't a ministerial preference, then as Christians, we should walk as directed by His instruction book. Make sure that this is what is being preached. I would also state before any of this is, to know who the leaders are before you follow. And, allow yourself that latitude. If the authorities within any system do not allow for this, then run for your life and your safety.

The result that can come from this type of totalistic church function is white washed-walls. Meaning, it looks nice and clean and shiny on the outside but on the inside, it is a different person or community, feeling, or reality. It can create great confusion for people. Especially for people who were raised within a cult church as a child. They

TOTALISM AND ELITISM

may grow up believing that if they subscribe to the preacher's "checklist" they must be o.k. before him (meaning the minister) which must make them o.k. before God and miss His real or first call, a call to brokenness before Him. There are thousands of children across America and across the globe that have been raised in these types of religious systems and left as adults with traumatic impacts. They are known as or called, "second-generation adults". And, many have never been able to unwrap the web of their experiences.

The Sweet

ALL THAT GLITTERS IS NOT GOLD!

When people walk the path of their religious experience or engagement, they are typically looking to better themselves or change some things or something about their path in life. They want to become a better person. They want to become closer to God or make peace with God. Or, they may want to contribute their life to the greater good and impact people for the better. Sometimes we are looking for a utopian community, society, or church. We look for what is appealing or looks attractive and may hold some promise of making a greater tomorrow for us and our lives. For some people, it may be the rigid lifestyle that is attractive in a church or religious system. Or, maybe it is a charismatic leader who has dynamic speaking or preaching ability and can move people in their hearts toward a greater common good. Or, it may be the love that congregants show to one another as they serve others or it may be a tight-knit family structure. Or, it may be the great outreach programs that are a part of the system or church.

Whatever the allurement or attraction point is that compels people to become a part of a religious system or church is what I call the "sweet" or the "candy". It is the driving force that compels people to devote their hearts to these same entities or bodies of people. These attractive points are things that they would look at at a glance and say, "that looks like a good thing" or "that is something I want to be a part of". But what they may not see or what they may not understand as a newcomer to a religious association is what is not readily visible or what is under the surface. This could be a rather large list. For instance: manipulative leaders who suppress information, physically or sexually abusive leaders, emotionally abusive leaders, totalistic leaders, warped scriptural teachings, pharisaical teachers and congregants, etc., etc. Whatever the sour in a church cult is, you may not recognize it till you are well on your way into it and vested. Further, the things that were of quality or sweet may make it difficult for people to see what is distorted or that it is rotten at the core.

This newly discovered "sour" or fraudulent functioning that has been captured into your mind for analysis can be a difficult thing to do especially if you have been 100% vested in the system. It may mean that, as you analyze this newly revealed information, that maybe you were a contributor to the dysfunction of the legalistic church or cult church that you are or were a part of. This can be a hard pill to swallow and can make you internally angry at yourself.

For me, I had to own my elitist mentality, isolationist functioning, judgmental spirit, sectarian stance, and shunning of people or avoidance of people who quite frankly, didn't deserve it. This was an extremely heavy weight for me to own as I turned and looked into the mirror of my own religious experience and functioning. It was painful and made me, as stated above, angry at me.

But, how could that happen to a God-fearing Christian? Who would ever want that on their spiritual resume? You guessed correctly! No one. Absolutely no one. If you would have tried to persuade me that I had any one of those above-stated characteristics before God revealed it to me, I would have strongly resisted any indictment. To the point of strong contention. But I would tell you that I was an open thinker or libertarian and that if there was anything out of place with my spiritual walk, please let me know. With the cloak unveiled and looking back at a clean or clearer rearview mirror today, I would have to say, I was not very open to considering much of anything. Most elitists aren't.

To show one of the more impacting examples of how alluring a religious system can be, I will use the example that often comes to my mind and even more so after having vacated the cult that I and my family were a part of. It is an example that would attract most, whether they are religious or

THE SWEET 41

not. When I was in my late teens or early twenties, The Church of Jesus Christ of Latter-Day Saints (Mormons) produced a captivating commercial. It was a commercial that would span most age categories as well as religious affiliations.

This is the Image that I still remember after almost 35 years and it was well done for the masses to recruit more congregants. Envision a series of rolling green hills and beautiful trees with a beautiful blue sky that hangs tuffets of clouds. Then, gracefully strolling along those beautiful hills is an absolutely beautiful and wholesome couple holding hands and a picnic basket and blanket. Then, while the Image of a beautiful life together is being depicted, in the background, the narrator with a soft and gentle voice says "life questions, we have answers". Ends with, "brought to you by The Church of Jesus Christ of Latter-Day Saints". The image that it imprints is saintly, meaning absolute purity.

For me, what I saw before I became a part of the church that I ultimately came to believe was a legalistic cult church was the wholesomeness amongst the families, children that were fairly well behaved, some good theological teaching, love expressed through serving one another, separation from the world and the list goes on. This was my sweet, this was my candy. Others may see or experience genuine friendships they never had before, a sense of purpose or belonging, a sense of superiority to others outside the group, and the comfort of blind obedience in which a person will no longer need to deal with making stressful decisions for themselves or family. What I did not see, what I did not grasp or capture in my understanding was the elitist mentality, the totalistic posture of its leaders, and the isolationist standard that separated itself from almost all outside entities. This is what I missed and didn't see till twenty-four years in.

So, with 26 years of being a culti and if there was ever any glory of being a part of a cult or a degree for cultic divinity, I earned it and learned it well. So, I'm going to write on, and I hope you read on as well.

Cults Across America and Around the World

The complexity of cults and their unique functioning can sometimes be readily identifiable although many can be more difficult to detect. In my opinion, those that would be more difficult to detect as a cult would be more along the lines of your fundamentalist style of church. Fundamentalism started in the late 1800s and early 1900s and was a Christian-based militant evangelical movement that started to oppose Protestant Liberalism and secularism or worldliness in the church. These churches were and still are today, typically characterized by an unwavering set of beliefs or dogmas. Rejection is typically the result of people who do not follow the belief system or challenge its dogmas. Also, they maintain a strong sense of maintaining ingroup and outgroup distinctions. Some of you who are reading this are possibly saying to yourself," what is wrong with following a biblical belief system"? There isn't! But, when the system pressures compliance and doesn't allow individuals to determine for themselves if it is accurate theologically and of value for their own life, then it (referring to the church) should be viewed as dogmatic and potentially dangerous.

Looking across the landscape of religious cultic systems in the United States as well as around the world we will find multiple flavors of Hinduism, Christianity, Mormonism, Adventism, and Muslims. There is no end to the buffet line of cults and religions. You can pick and choose your favorite flavor that you identify with. Foundationally most forms of religion or cults want to be a representation or a path to a better or more moral lifestyle that seeks after God. But, unfortunately, in the midst of the moral value or values system are elements that can: distort the view of who God is, make congregants feel devalued by authoritarian leaders, individuals can become whitewashed, separate you from family and friends, isolate you from normal social functioning, become a slave to the merry go round of cultic function, distort your view of others, distort the scriptures, create extreme views and beliefs by wrapping the scriptures around a preferential belief system.

So, onto the big question! Why would someone join a cult? Well, the fact of the matter is, most people if not all would never join a cult. But, on an initial observance of a functioning religious body of people, the new convert or potentially new convert will be looking for the positive benefits or a way to develop and advance their life for the better. In the new congregant's life, these newly found beliefs or practices, in their thinking, will serve to advance them. They are looking at what it can do for them as an individual. The downfall for most people who become a part of a cult is that the positive attributes can overshadow the destructive functioning or ideologies. This is a great paradox; people want to better themselves but may be ultimately walking down a path of mental distress or even physical destruction. Once an individual may see the light that they were or are a part of a cult and then extract themselves, then this is where another form of destruction or anguish of heart may begin. The individual may look back and begin to become angry toward God and others who they may now see as individuals that harmed them or others. With this new panoramic view, the anger that is projected by the individual toward God may be feelings that are related to, their thinking: why didn't God protect me, why didn't God show me that it was a cult, why did he allow me to be sexually abused or physically abused, why did He abandon me while I was within, why did He lead me to be a part of this system, why did he allow the system's ideology to separate me from my family, etc., etc. The flood of emotions that come from these thoughts can become overpowering and the individual may become isolated. They may feel embarrassed to share their struggle with anyone since their trust level at this point is minimal, if any, toward anyone and rightfully so.

In the American view of cults, we will almost always view them as malevolent, meaning that they willingly injure or inflict pain on their members or force their views on their congregants in a very dogmatic approach. The cults that typically make the headlines in the news are malevolent ones. In my opinion, most are not malevolent but inadvertently inflict emotional pain or trauma. As you read on, I will present five different cults with multiple facets of structure but also some functions of similarities.

1. **Jim Jones and The People's Temple**: Possibly recognized as the most popular or most well-known cult in history and also lending itself to free advertisement for Kool Aide. This cult initially was a charismatic fundamentalist style of a church with a very alluring leader who stood against social injustices for the black community. This was a drawing card for many black people

in Indianapolis, Indiana, and Oakland, CA., and surrounding communities in the California area and was the launching ground for Jim Jones's vision for the future. Jim Jones in his early years of life, never really felt accepted and as he attended church and viewed the communities around him, he noticed or felt sympathy for the black community as he witnessed many black people in his hometown not being accepted as well. This stirred emotions in him that he could relate with. This spurred him to be a vicar for social injustice issues which ultimately drew the black community to him and the church he was a minister of. Unfortunately, the more power he got, the more power he wanted. One of his methods of drawing an individual in was to identify what was most important to the individual and then use that as a way or means to make new converts feel like he had a genuine interest in them. Beyond his social justice crusades, he as well as the People's Temple, were great at outreach to a community of needs. Some of the ways that they served in the community were through their drug and alcohol rehab center, a senior care center, a daycare center, and a soup kitchen. Many people became a part of this cult church through these outreach efforts. Many of society's hurting, damaged or disenfranchised found a place of belonging through these different community efforts. Jim was also a master of making himself look saintly to his cause of social integration. He did this by adopting, along with his wife, multiple children from different races. This set the stage to make him look like he practiced what he preached in the area of social integration. He also preached that sexual proclivity was acceptable for the furthering of God's Kingdom, I mean Jim's kingdom. To bring his view of unity and obedience together, he would go as far as public ridicule and public (meaning in the church) beatings to instill fear in people that he was not to be crossed or challenged. He also instilled through the public ministry the fear of dictatorial rule in the United States becoming a reality. This is the fear that ultimately drove him and his followers to leave the United States and establish their isolated and closed society in Guyana. This ultimately created a mounting concern for family members who lived back in the U.S. and they urged politicians to investigate this mass exodus of congregants and their newly found and seemingly developed mecca. In November 1978, U.S. Congressman Leo Ryan traveled to Guyana to inspect the Peoples Temple's activities and the Jonestown commune. He was investigating rumors that some members of the cult were being held against their will and that some were being subjected to physical and psychological abuse. After traveling to Guyana's capital, Georgetown, on November 14, he arrived at Jonestown on November 17. The following day, when Ryan was set to return home, several Temple members who wanted to leave the compound boarded his delegation's truck to accompany him back to the United States. Ryan was stabbed shortly before the vehicle left the compound, but he escaped, and the truck continued with Ryan aboard along with several journalists. Temple members then launched an attack at the airstrip from which Ryan and his company were to depart. Five people, including Ryan and three members of the press, were shot and killed, and 11 others were wounded. In the wake of the shooting, Jones released radio orders for Temple members outside the compound to commit suicide. In previous years Jones had conducted a "mock" mass suicide with congregants. Shortly thereafter Jones enacted his plan at the compound, which members had "practiced" in the past, in which a fruit drink was laced with cyanide, tranquilizers, and sedatives. It was first squirted into the mouths of babies and children via syringes and then drank by adult members. Jones himself died of a gunshot wound. Fewer than 100 of the Temple members in Guyana survived the massacre; the majority of survivors either had defected that day or were in Georgetown. Officials later discovered a cache of firearms, hundreds of passports stacked together, and $500,000 in U.S. currency. Millions more had reportedly been deposited in bank accounts overseas. The Peoples Temple effectively disbanded after the incident and declared bankruptcy at the end of 1978. After reading some of the structural characteristics of the People's Temple, do you see some of the sweet, meaning the drawing card? When I say sweet, I am not giving any glory to Jim Jones. I'm simply hoping you can see the aspects that were positive or of benefit to people: a drug rehab center, senior care center, child care, standing up for social injustices, and a soup kitchen. The Sweet!

2. **NXIVM** was one of our society's more recent cults to step into the public or media spotlight. This is a cult with a whole different twist that leaves the bible and God out of the picture. But, strongly sets out to develop individuals and their stature in society through self-help seminars. Foundationally, it was founded as a multilevel marketing company. Twisted? You bet! Through the early indoctrination process or onboarding, the leaders would tap into or draw out new converts' deep dark pains or secrets. Only to later be used against them if they threatened to leave or challenged Keith or the leadership. Keith Raineere along with his sidekick and confidant, Nancy Sulzman, that helped to launch him to his iconic level was a charismatic leader who shared his wisdom with his followers that they together with

him could build an ethical nonviolent world. They also had a very consistent or regular number of events that were like summer camps on steroids that were designed to stimulate a high arousal level in the attendees. Sounds good to me. Sounds kind of sweet! Along with his charismatic charm, he was also able to allure women to this organization through a program that they taught, called Jness. It was a program that was described or advertised as a process to liberate or free women and empower them. And, that women had the right to feel what they want to feel. With this allurement that appealed to the women who would follow him, would also come Keith's love bombing to both men and women. It was common after his seminars, to embrace and kiss on the lips, one by one, each of the participants that attended these events. This was the foundation to desensitize those that he would use for his sexual gratification. What most of his followers did not know was that he was a convicted child molester. Do you think that his followers would believe it if they found out about it? Would they minimize it or deny it without even looking into it? This or any other higher-profile accusation should always be considered or looked into when it is an individual who exercises authority or responsibility over people. It is a safeguard to protect people and determine genuine integrity or if the individual is potentially dangerous. In this case, he was not only dangerous, but he was also a narcissist that had himself filmed constantly. He felt that he was going to leave his mark on history, so what better way than to film himself as a living walking history book through cinematography. Financially, most of the money that was used to sustain this cult was from the heiresses of Seagram's liquor. The amount of money that they contributed to this organization is higher than most of us can count. It was further supported by pressuring individuals to sell their assets and then contribute them to NXIVM to go further within the organization. And yes, there were fees along with multi-level marketing as part of their program. Ultimately, he was convicted of child sex trafficking, sex offenses, racketeering, and forced labor. His sentence was 120 years. Give thanks!

3. **The Farm** was a communal living, hippie-based movement that spawned out of the Haight-Ashbury district of San Francisco and was founded in 1971. Their foundation was based on a bible verse, Acts 2:44, which reads; and all the believers met together in one place and shared everything they had. Their core beliefs were taught by Stephen Gaskins who was their Guru. He taught a mixture of eastern religions combined with Christianity. Some of their bylaws were:

abstinence from alcohol, no birth control, no tobacco use, they were vegetarians, nonviolent, showed respect for the earth, shared what they grew collectively, leaned toward premarital abstinence, were not allowed to be angry, promoted marriage, in some earlier beliefs they allowed for four-way marriage, believed in smoking a lot of marijuana, took a vow of poverty and abstained from man-made drugs. Although, many of them had used psychedelic drugs which initially aided in the development of their belief system and communal structure. Some claimed to have had a collective psychedelic experience that gave them a vision for the future of their movement. Before being allowed to become a member of the farm, they had to sign a vow or agreement to these bylaws. Although their movement spawned out of the Haight-Ashbury district, they ultimately came to reside in central Tennessee to set down roots and live collectively. Initially, their commune was founded by roughly three hundred people and ultimately grew as large as sixteen hundred people. Eventually, they purchased 1064 acres for $70.00 each. Not a bad deal. Shortly after, they purchased an additional 750 acres for $100 each. Their ultimate goal or end game was to create a better world through universal brotherhood. Today, the Farm is composed of roughly 200 residents that are primarily descendants of those who initially established the movement. Many of them have established their own businesses to sustain themselves in a more viable method. They were also very instrumental in bringing back or establishing our modern-day midwifery. When you look at some of their ideas or structure, do you see anything attractive? Anything sweet? Maybe for you, you see nothing attractive but for that generation, it had some attractive points. There was some allurement.

4. **The Children of God** or later known as the Family of Love was spawned in southern California in the 1960s and eventually grew to roughly 10,000 members across 76 countries. David Berg was its founder and was an evangelist whose roots were founded or developed by his parents in the Pentecostal movement. His early experiences with his parents were abusive physically and sexually. Yet, at the same time, his parents would shame him for his self-exploration. This incestuous behavior was the foundation that ultimately led him to justify his latter functioning or structure for the way people of all ages were abused sexually in his cult. Contraception was banned and since there were no boundaries between married couples, many children were conceived that were not from the husband that the woman was married to. David Berg, also known

as Moses David, called this sexual freedom among its congregants, "sharing". One of their evangelical tools was to produce music videos of the young congregants dancing in a very synchronized manner. These videos were used to allure others to see a wholesomeness amongst their youth and hopefully entice families on the outside to become interested in who they were. The youth would also evangelize door-to-door and business-to-business. Berg's ultimate goal was world conquest. He also excessively focused on preaching about the end times and set the date of Christ's return in 1993. He took control of new converts' assets and had them give up their careers to have them fulfill his purposes. To further his evangelical strength, he preached that women should use sex as a method to lure men to the fold. He called this "flirty fishing". To further his grip, reading books was viewed as worldly and should be forbidden. The congregants were also discouraged from taking any medicine. It was viewed as a sign of weakness. The most unbelievable aspect about Berg is that most of the congregants never saw or met him. He was in constant hiding. The congregation's only source of communication with him was through videos that he produced of himself along with letters that he wrote, called the "Mo" letters. From these two mediums, they received their walking orders for function. These "Mo" letters often were written in a cartoon format and were often pornographic. Through his processes, he was able to desensitize his followers sexually. Ultimately, stripping was practiced in front of congregants by both women young and old, and sex between adults and young people was acceptable. The height of depravity. Fortunately, David Berg died in 1995 and left a wake of destruction in his path of totalistic abuse, only to leave the reins of the cult in his first wife's hands. Unfortunately, it is still functional today but with far fewer members. The amount of traumatic pain that remains in the lives of former members is over the top and is further reason that I am writing this book in hopes to help others.

5. **Scientology or Dianetics**, founded by L. Ron Hubbard in the 1950s, was initially spawned or brought forth as an organization that was founded on the modern science of mental health. Eventually, it metamorphosized in time to become a church with ordained ministers and is registered with the IRS, and has a 501-c3 status. This means they are tax-exempt. Scientology operates hundreds of churches and missions around the world. This is where new converts receive most of their introductory training. These churches are licensed franchises. In other words, they are a church that is a business

that is tax exempt. How underhanded is that? One of the largest of these church franchises is based in Hollywood. This was established by design for two reasons: the first was to raise capital and the second was to gain public attention for new converts through the proselytization of the Hollywood elite. Therapeutic counseling of an individual's prior traumas is a focus. The purpose is to free individuals of past experiences through psychotherapy. Hubbard called it modern-day spiritual healing technology. These healing sessions cost these new converts hundreds of dollars per hour. Many people who became a part of this organization applied these techniques to other new converts to help and free them from their past traumas as well. In essence, many of the Scientologists function as clinical therapists without the credentials. Many of their beliefs are not made public but will be revealed little by little to its members once enough money transfers hands. Some of the foundational beliefs are that man is immortal, and that they can heal and improve themselves with their own strength. They also believe that past traumas can come from former lives dating back millions of years. Scientology's aim was to, through its practices, create a civilization without insanity, without criminals, and without war. Further, Scientology imposes no particular view of God but allows its followers the opportunity to discover God through their teaching as the individual applies them to their life. Within the structure of this organization are leaders who regulate ethics and make sure that those who do not comply are held accountable. They also staff a special affairs intelligence agency that targets those who are critics of the church. This church has also made multiple efforts to infiltrate government at multiple levels. And, harasses people who are perceived as enemies of the church, and its current top leader, David Miscavige, has denied allegations from his staff that he has been at times physically abusive and demoralizing toward them. When I look at some of the things they stand for, I would say they look like attractive points for many to want to be a part of. When I look at some of their processes for operation or function, I say run for your life.

Of the five cults that were presented above, they each had at least one of the three aspects that are commonly part of a cult's structure. And, that is elitism, isolationism, and totalism. At this point, writing about these five different versions of what I deem as cults, I'm feeling a little emotionally drained and you may be as well. Let's move on to the next chapter.

Groupthink!

What do you think? What do I think? Well, quite frankly it doesn't matter what you think. What matters is that you think as the group thinks. Or, you need to think as I think. Or else, you'll be viewed as one on the outside. But I want to be on the inside. So then, comply. I know what you are thinking now. You think I stole this straight out of one of DR. Seuss's books?

In a nutshell, in the above paragraph, I have laid the foundation of "Groupthink". In essence, it is a subtle version of mind control or brainwashing. When any environment pressures universal conformity, then it translates to universal thinking or mindsets. Although many religious or cultic organizations do not intentionally brainwash, they in their efforts to conform individuals to the group's views inadvertently do this. Over time, with this process, cult members or people who are a part of a legalistic church system give up more control to the leadership and develop an identity that is paralleled to the values of the group or religious system. The identity that may have once been a part of their life has now been chipped away, little by little.

With groupthink, many people will set aside their personal beliefs or adopt the opinions of the rest of the group. Those who have opposing views of the group's thinking or have a strong opinion frequently remain silent. In a cult or religious association, these individuals prefer to keep peace rather than shake the uniformity of the group. These people can be well-intentioned, but because of pressure from group thinking, they can ultimately make bad choices.

Groupthink may not always be easy to discern, but there are typically some signs that it is present. There are also some situations where it may be more likely to occur. The list below will help you identify more effectively whether this is something that is a part of your religious function currently or in the past. Or, it may be something that is happening with a friend or family member.

- **Illusions of unity** leads members to believe that everyone is in agreement and feels the same way. It is often much more difficult to speak out when it seems that everyone else in the group is on the same page.

- **Unquestioned beliefs** lead members to ignore possible moral problems and not consider the consequences of individual and group actions.

- **Rationalizing** prevents members from reconsidering their beliefs and causes them to ignore warning signs.

- **Stereotyping** leads members of the in-group to ignore or even demonize out-group members who may oppose or challenge the group's ideas. This causes members of the group to ignore important ideas or information.

- **Self-censorship** causes people who might have doubts to hide their fears or misgivings. Rather than sharing what they know, people remain quiet and assume that the group must know best.

- **Mind guards** act as self-appointed censors to hide problematic information from the group. Rather than sharing important information, they keep quiet or actively prevent sharing.

- **Illusions of invulnerability** lead members of the group to be overly optimistic and engage in risk-taking. When no one speaks out or voices an alternative opinion, it causes people to believe that the group must be right.

- **Direct pressure** to conform is often placed

on members who pose questions, and those who question the group are often seen as disloyal or traitors.[1]

Because most people that are a part of a cult, legalistic church, or religious system don't want to disrupt harmony or be ill-thought of or feel rejected, they will continue their functioning with silence. This type of function is more common in associations where individuals are similar. When the leader is more charismatic in these types of associations and has the respect or blessing of the congregants, then dissent becomes even riskier. This type of structure will compel congregants to feel a strong need for group identity. Another issue that groupthink can create is inefficient problem-solving for religious affiliations. This can be further complicated by the fact that the average age of cult members is twenty-five years old. And, this has not allowed their years of experience in critical thinking development.

---

1. www.verywellmind.com

These issues that arise from groupthink are not only a part of some religious or cultic organizations but are also a part of educational systems, political systems, dictatorial governments, and military systems. It is not unique to cults or religious affiliations.

So, you say you have something you want to express now. Then say it!

If expressing something within your religious affiliation, that is not a part of the ideological thought or function for consideration and it is not allowed or suppressed or chided or minimized or receives a degrading response, then establish a boundary that you will not allow others to cross. And that is, suppressing your expression of thought will not be tolerated or exit stage left.

The Rebuilding Process

LIFE WILL KNOCK YOU DOWN MORE TIMES THAN YOU CAN POSSIBLY IMAGINE

When exiting a cult, a person can become overwhelmed or almost paralyzed with anger when they see the damage that was done by themselves or the destructively religious system and ideology or by other congregants and leaders. The extent of damage can cross over into multiple aspects of a person's life. They may have alienated immediate family or extended family. This may have occurred through excessive isolation, not participating in funerals, holidays, or missing birthdays. Another aspect that it may have created is alienation between former cult members and family that were on the outside, are the extreme views that were held, believed, or projected on these family members. These dynamics can stir the family pot and create a lot of unsettled issues between families.

Going beyond the family issues, the former cult member may reflect on aspects of employment opportunities that were viewed in the cultic ideology as not acceptable or potentially risky and as result, left their place of employment or opportunities only to settle for something less than adequate. This same thinking can be paralleled in the area of education. For instance, college or the public school system may represent in the cultic ideology, "a place where worldliness abounds", so it becomes marginalized as a nonviable place to be educated. This may in turn equate to settling for an education that is minimal at best or only allows for some type of trade. Or, it may limit or ultimately reduce their future career to cult-owned and or operated businesses.

THE REBUILDING PROCESS

This can be further compounded when the former cult member sees that they had limited opportunities to be participants in extracurricular activities. This is because the cultic ideas view participation as possibly worldly or a bad influence. So, families and or children may not participate in any athletics outside their realm or they may not participate in any community-sponsored or religiously sponsored outreach efforts.

What I have explained in the three paragraphs above is Isolationism. The definition is as follows: a doctrine or policy of minimal participation to avoid becoming entangled or influenced by outside entities.

We all need to make decisions for ourselves and set proper boundaries for ourselves as relates to where we are willing to participate when it comes to school, education, employment choices, family interaction, and what extracurricular activities to participate in or become a part of. If these processes are given heavy guidance by a religious leader or system, it can break down one's ability to make wise choices for themselves or their family.

It can minimize individuality and also thwart adult decision-making processes. When individuals learn to make wise choices as a result of former decision-making processes that were ultimately made on their own along with sought-after input, this can create an adult who has critical thinking skills that can navigate life more effectively.

O.K., so at this point, whether you are reading for educational purposes or because you are a current or former cult church member who wants to develop, you may be just a bit overwhelmed and wonder if recovery from all this is possible. One of the greatest and most effective ways to transition from a legalistic church or cult status to safer ground is to have a place to land after your departure. What I mean is, before you leave, try to find a community that you can begin to interact in or be a part of. For instance, my wife and I made a lot of effort to be active in civic/faith-based outreach. We also made efforts to develop relationships with members of the churches that we started to attend as well. Or, look for an athletic league that you would like to be a part of. If you like music, look for a local ensemble that you can play music with. If you like books, join a book club. If you bike ride, join a bike club. If you like art or academics, sign up for classes at the local community college. You get the point, don't isolate yourself all over again. You may not find relationships that click immediately. Give yourself time and latitude to find mutually satisfying relationships that will work for you. Don't force them. They will come in time. Initially, you may feel a little bit awkward or unsure of yourself and where you stand in the new network that you are trying to establish. Remember that you are perfectly loveable, and other people need to be loved as well.

A couple of other issues that may need to be considered are a new place of residency or possibly a new job. You may need to move as far away as possible from the system that gripped your soul for your safety. If you are a woman with children who has not had a job because of caring for a child or children or you are someone who was abused or someone who has no funds because it was taken from you for the cult's use, then there is a path out to safety. If your family members who you may have alienated yourself from are open to helping you, this may be a good first stop for you. If this is not a viable path and there has been abuse inflicted on you by cultic leaders or members, contact law enforcement. Also, if you were to do a Google search in your local area, you will probably find multiple abuse hotlines or organizations. You may find several that come up that are very willing to help you through your traumatic recovery and regain a life of solid ground. They should be able to give guidance, help, or support. They have been trained to do this. If income or a job is needed, typically people who come out of cults are hard workers. This is the result of living a regimented lifestyle and can be an asset to a new employer on the outside. If you are with children and have no one to help support you financially, multiple government assistance programs can provide monetary support, housing, or food. It simply requires you to apply and explain your current situation. Asking for help, if you are a giver, may require some humility on your part to seek help till you can figure out how

THE REBUILDING PROCESS

to stabilize on your own two feet. It is reported that 42% of people who leave cults, do it covertly by sneaking out at night. This means that there is a lot of risk to the individual and lends credence to the importance of having a place to land and a plan. Meaning a place of protection. When local authorities or outside entities have been minimized or criticized frequently, this can make it difficult for the individual who wants to depart to reach out for help. This can create a mental quandary for the departing cult member and requires those who are helping them once on the outside to be gentle in their approach as if helping an individual coming out of a war-torn zone and is seriously injured.

To The Forgotten Family Members

In my opinion, the family members that are connected directly to members of cults are the ones that seem to be overlooked when it comes to pain and trauma. This pain and trauma can be linked to their loved one's cultic journey and dogmatic adherence to their newly found path in life. Me, I was oblivious to the pain that I would inflict on my family that I left behind. I was completely focused on my newly found ideals with really no latitude for much of anything or anybody. My goals were different, my friends were different, and my thought process became black and white with pretty much everything. Seemingly, the cult provided me with a new family and a culture of rules that encapsulated me in my day-to-day life. Looking back, I think part of me looked at the church cult that I had become a part of, as a vehicle that could do something for me. Something to better myself.

Many who leave a cult, become haunted by PTSD (post-traumatic stress disorder). They become flooded with anger, disappointment, self-doubt, low self-worth, losses, religious confusion, and bitterness toward the world and the life they had lived through. The hand they were dealt, in their thinking, does not line up with the life that they felt that they deserved or that the cult should have provided. Likewise, family members who were left behind on the outside of the church cult may also have suffered from PTSD. For ex-cult members as well as their families that were left behind (meaning on the outside), it may take a couple of years or more to work through the pain, emotions, and issues to come to a place of more stable ground in the relationship and life in general.

For those of you who have looked on at a friend or family member that has had to stand by, so to speak, as they watched their loved one enter and then stay absorbed into a cult, then please have a heart full of compassion for them. Because the following may very well be what is happening in their heart and mind:

- Feel that they have lost them for good.

- Questioned their relationship with them.

- Have self-doubt about how they raised their child.

- Become lonely as a result of them no longer being present.

- Pained by their family members not being a part of family functions or holidays.

- Embarrassed before others because those who are close to them are aware of their family member's current cultic entry or experience.

- May beat themselves up mentally due to previous interactions or conversations that did not end well with the family member before becoming a part of the cult.

- Spiral into a deep dark mental hole when they realize there may be nothing they can do to extract them.

For me, I can only imagine what my parents felt or experienced. I think that they probably felt that it was just a passing phase that I would grow out of. Unfortunately, for them as well as for me, I did not grow out of it but continued to be a part of the church cult that I was a part of for twenty-six years. In retrospect, I believe my mother was the one who was primarily hurt. I think she felt rejected or abandoned by me as I very abruptly stopped attending most family functions as well as all holiday functions. And to further the distance, I moved to the other side of the country. And, over twenty-two years I would fly back across the country to visit every two to three years. When I look back, it makes my own heart sad for my losses as well as for my children's loss as relates to lack of interaction with family members.

Ultimately, after leaving the cult church, I returned home to my homeland of Northern California. My goal was to be a help to my mother who was ailing and if possible, reconnect with family members. My mother received me with arms of grace and kindness as well as my older sister. For this, I am forever grateful. And, unfortunately, with other family members, they've kept their distance. And, I am to blame for this. I don't blame them. So, what can you do if you or someone you know is in or was in a cultic or religiously abusive situation? This is what I would suggest:

- Despite the pain, you may have experienced, show grace to the individual.

- Try to understand that there was or is a powerful force in the life of the cult member or former cult member that may have rocked their world as well as yours.

- If they still have some cultic views, do not try to fix them or straighten them out. In time they may come to see what you see.

- Be the rock in the relationship. In other words, if they are open to interacting with you, pursue them to participate in activities. Be the one they can come to when they are troubled, down, lonely, etc.

- Do not press them to open up or discuss their religious views, current or former.

- Allow time for the relationship to flow more openly and at this point, you may find that they will be willing to open up.

Many people in the United States as well as around the globe have been a victim of a cult or cult church either directly or indirectly. Cults are prevalent around the world and will continue to be. It is reported or estimated that more than 2.5

million people in the past 40 years have been a part of a cult in the U.S. That is no small number. What that amplifies to me is that there are a lot of people who have been impacted and need help. Although this country offers a lot in the way of therapists, in my experience/research, there are very few cultic counselors. When a Google search is done to find cult counselors, you will find them titled "exit counselors". Although these types of counselors may have a lot to offer, my fear or concern is, how many counselors really understand the dynamics of destructive forces that a cult can permeate into the core of someone's soul. And, as expressed previously, have they as a counselor ever experienced being a part of a cult themselves?

Cults And Law Enforcement

To begin with, I do not claim to be an expert on law enforcement and how they should handle extreme cults. This subject is complex and I won't even scratch the surface. But I do have some personal views and enough understanding of cults and what stirs in the core of some of their belief systems. With many in our current generation, we reflect on The Branch Davidians and the high-profile law enforcement raid that ended in absolute destruction. Ultimately, The Davidian's compound burned to the ground along with twenty adults and fourteen children. Autopsies performed afterward revealed that they all had been shot, children included. Although this story is very heartbreaking and gruesome, it has multiple facets to be considered from the perspective of law enforcement as well as from those who were residents of the Waco, Texas compound. It was also called by the Davidians, Mount Carmel. In short, the Branch Davidians were an offshoot of Seventh-Day Adventism. They were founded or originated in 1955 by Victor Houteff. Victor was a prophetic minister that strongly focused on the apocalypse and the end times. After Victor's death, the leadership or ministry fell into the hands of his widow, Florence Houteff. When her deceased husband's prophesied date of Armageddon and Christ's return failed, then she became marginalized and Benjamin Roden was the new leader. When Benjamin died then his wife became the new leader and ultimately groomed Vernon Howell as her successor, later renaming himself David Koresh. It was in the early to mid-80s that Koresh rose to power. He, as well as his predecessors, saw himself as a profit of end times. He had oversight over multiple, multigenerational families, meaning raised from within. He in time was able to dictate the celibacy of the other husbands and then assume the new role of siring their wives. He also promoted excessive fear of government and law enforcement. In his sermons, at times, he would educate his flock on the proper use of firearms. Ultimately, a neighboring farmer became concerned when he heard the excessive use or training with machine guns on the Davidian property. He shared or reported his concerns to local officials. This prompted concerns on the part of federal authorities, which led to a search warrant being issued for suspected possession of illegal firearms. When the ATF began communicating with Koresh on February 28, 1993, this began to set the stage for Koresh to assume control and have the attention of the world to feed his narcissistic needs. When the ATF initially tried to enter the compound, they were met with fierce firearm resistance which led to four ATF agents being killed and sixteen being injured. This was the beginning of a fifty-one-day standoff that would change history forever. It also created a vacuum of information for law enforcement to consider for any future dealings with cults. The end result being: multiple law enforcement officials being killed or injured, multiple children shot and burned to death as well as multiple other adult Davidians dying in the process of the attempted siege. I would have to say that the Federal authorities as well as the local authorities had to have taken a second look at their processes when or after the standoff finally ended. The carnage was devastating and left a mental imprint as many Americans watched the compound burn to the ground. They were mesmerized by the inferno that engulfed the Davidian compound. If there was ever a cult that left a taste of shock and awe for us to remember, it was the Davidian cult. The whole event was perilous and left its mark on history forever

When law enforcement began to consider how to work with managing or dealing with the Davidians, they did have some initial thoughts of trying to capture David Koresh while he was outside of the Davidian compound and in town taking care of business. They also had some history and knowledge of the cult from previous experiences

CULTS AND LAW ENFORCEMENT

with some of its members. Unfortunately, this idea got pushed aside. To me, it would have been the best choice. It would have allowed the opportunity to separate him from his followers and not allow him the time or opportunity to give directives to his flock. I believe it would have also left many people alive today.

When authorities are informed of illegal or questionable cultic conduct, they should in my opinion treat it as if they were being called into a domestic dispute. In other words, approach with extreme caution. Law enforcement has a wide variety of codes that they will often use when they communicate or receive walking orders from dispatch. For instance: 10-0 means "use caution" and 10-30 means "danger/caution". This is exactly the way any cult should be perceived. That being said, I am not implying that they are all irrational and dangerous. The utmost caution should be used just as if they were dealing with a domestic abuse dispute that was reported to have physical abuse present. When law enforcement arrives, to deal with a domestic dispute it can greatly escalate emotions and then danger can ensue rapidly and become out of control. Likewise, when authorities are called upon to deal with any cult, it can also exasperate or escalate feelings toward authority. This is especially true for cults that have been taught to view or minimize the credibility or viability of law enforcement just like the Davidians. In reality, law enforcement may be playing Russian roulette with leaders or individuals who have a belief set that tells them in their thinking: they are doing God's will, they are God's only true representatives on earth, their walking order or dogma has come directly from God and the dogma may include resistance to governing authorities. This means if they are playing Russian roulette with authorities then they are willing to take the bullet with little fear since they are doing God's will and fulfilling his purpose for his kingdom. This type of belief set serves the core of a cult leader's soul or his follower's soul to know that they may become a martyr for their mission that came directly from God. Beware!

Children Raised From Within

Sad to say thousands and thousands of children have been raised from birth within a cult or legalistic church system. It further saddens me that I raised my three children from within a cult as well. My wife was also born and raised within the same cult where we raised our three children. This foundation of religious experience and early indoctrination can be a web that is difficult to escape mentally and physically. The sense of security that can surround the individual who is raised from within can be a driving factor that can keep them planted or remain rooted in the environment. This can be true regardless of bad experiences from within. There is a sense of security in having a consistent community, consistent family interaction, common goals, common views, the same religious ideals or belief system, etc., etc. This sense of security can cause them to remain within the system that they were fostered in from their youth and can be further cemented when they are trained to believe that there is no viable or functional life on the outside. They may have a sense of paranoia toward the outside world that may grip them with fear of ever leaving.

For the individual to leave after having reached adulthood, they will need to be strong of heart. Launching into a whole new world or experience can be frightening and unstabilizing for former cult members. As expressed in the previous chapter, they will also need to have a place to plant their feet. A solid community that can help them through their experience, former cult members that can resonate with their story, a family that was on the outside that can show them grace, or possibly a new church.

CHILDREN RAISED FROM WITHIN

Within time, the newly departed individual may experience a lot of internal turmoil as they look back on their upbringing. As they begin to look back at their childhood experiences, they may struggle with sorting out and understanding their old reality as well as their new reality. The reason this can be difficult to unravel or unlock is that when they look back at their childhood, they may see multiple aspects of their life that were good and positive experiences and may even agree with some of the beliefs that were fostered in them while young. This can create a mental dilemma. And, if the individual does not find viable life to function in or be a part of on the outside and still has cultic ties or relationships, they may return to function within the system they were raised in.

Unfortunately, childhood is what we may spend the rest of our lives trying to overcome or unwrap even if we were not raised in a cult or abusive religious system. It just creates one more layer of mental complexity to unwrap. For some, their experience in a religious system may have been so over the top and destructive that they want nothing to do with God or religion. Or, their experience may create a wave of tremendous anger toward God and debilitate the relationship that was once had with God. For some, these post-exit points can become further exacerbated by drug and alcohol abuse which can further complicate an individual's ability to unwrap the web of their past. Or, to see more clearly how their past makes them tick as relates to the new life that they are beginning to live. You may be saying to yourself that this is complicated. Well, you are correct. This is why it is extremely important to show grace to those who have come out of a cult. Be sensitive to their story if they are willing to share it.

An individual's experience can become further complicated while unraveling their legalistic cult church upbringing if they were physically abused. As an individual looks back and tries to assess why they were physically abused or try to make sense of it and they remember in retrospect that it was administered (referring to the physical abuse) due to their lack of compliance to religious ideals, then this can be termed spiritual abuse. When pressured compliance is administered within a legalistic church system or any religious system to comply with the culture, rules, or systematic beliefs, then this can potentially set the stage for abuse within a home. Let me explain. When the format or characteristic of public ministry or preaching rebukes individuals or publicly minimizes individuals or families for lack of compliance to the value system that is predominately adhered to by the cult church, then this can further equate to the pressure of compliance from parents to children. If this creates tension between the child and parents, and compliance by the child is not delivered, then potentially this can lead to physical abuse to create or coerce compliance. All in an effort for an individual or family to avoid public ridicule or to be perceived as Godly. Are you sick at this point? I am! And it disturbed me to write it.

Extremity of Doctrine

In many religious circles, whether they are Christian-based, Muslims, Jehovah's Witnesses, Mormons, Buddhists, or Seventh Day Adventists, in some instances project certain passages of scripture to the extreme, or an excessive amount of time is spent preaching about them. I call these their pet doctrines or beliefs that they lock onto like a Pitbull with a piece of meat. There are problems that this can create in individuals who are subject to this type of excessive focus. For instance, if the balance of the scriptures in a religious organization is overly focused on certain passages of scripture, then they may be missing other passages that can either balance, complement, or temper the excessive belief set or extreme view. For instance, my experiences while communicating with Seventh-Day Adventists have been typically focused on their set of views about food, health, the sabbath, and Jewish law. Also, my experiences when communicating with Jehovah's Witnesses have been a pretty consistent focus on the holidays and paganism, the deity of Christ, and the 144 thousand people mentioned in the book of Revelation. I have also had multiple experiences of communicating with people in charismatic circles or the "holiness movement" and they typically want to talk about or discuss the second blessings, meaning spiritual healing or speaking in tongues. The church cult that I was a part of, was no exception to this. We had subjects that I would call pet doctrines as well, that were not balanced by the whole word of God. Some of these were preached so strongly and consistently that there was almost no possibility for an individual to walk away with a tempered view that considered other scriptures. This would channel people down a path of little to no latitude. This would also create or develop in people a "groupthink" posture that would not allow latitude for others to choose a path of life or decision that was different from others in the church cult. It would at times and a lot of the time create a group mentality that would question the spiritual temperature of others if they did not adhere to the sermon that was being ministered. It did not leave much latitude for people to breathe and walk freely. Quite frankly, we lived in each other's back pockets. This fostered or created a judgmental spirit about us that blinded us to see our own set of scriptural violations. This was the problem the Pharisees had. And that is, they could see everyone else's set of issues or noncompliance but could not see their own hypocritical, non-compliant standards that were not being applied in their own lives, that were right under their noses.

As I look back at some of our own church cult pet doctrines that were ministered consistently and or excessively, I would have to say it was overly focused on a woman's walk. What I mean is they were overly subjected to preaching that was focused on: clothing and modesty, headship and submission, and hair and adornment. Some of these doctrines were our identity, so to speak. In my evaluation or opinion, these subjects were ministered so excessively, that it was probably 25%-35% of the ministerial focus of preaching. If I were a lady, I would feel like I could never measure up, never satisfy God, never feel accepted or approved by God, or others, or never satisfy my husband. If you take the combined total of each of the subjects above, that are addressed in the scriptures, they take up about one page in the Bible. The Bible is composed of hundreds and hundreds of pages and leaves me to conclude that the balance or ratio of these subjects was preached in excess concerning the overall depth of subjects that are or were available to be preached by the cult church I was a part of or any other church.

For me, or any other man, the subject of headship and submission was an attractive subject to hear preached by the minister, especially as a young man. Just like a woman likes to hear when a minister reads or preaches that a man is to love his wife like Christ loved the church and that he should cherish her and

EXTREMITY OF DOCTRINE

not treat her harshly. These are good qualities for a man to apply. Unfortunately, I think men tend to be overly focused on the wife's spiritual walk. And what I mean is, we can be quick to point out any inconsistency of a woman as pertains to this passage. This is ineffective and can, in my view, be verbally or emotionally abusive. Unfortunately, as a younger man, I would at times point this out to my wife, only to leave her hurting and misunderstood. Fortunately, I learned my role was to walk before Christ and not demand or express a lack of submission. A woman's walk and or role is her choice and decision before God. Not mine or any other person's.

At this point, I think many of you who have read this far are blown away by the complex and subtle aspects of cults, religions, or legalistic churches. You may feel like you have been manipulated by religious family members or religious leaders that have led you to a life that has given you a gaping hole that needs to be filled, answers that need to be had, and a heart that desperately needs to be healed. The following chapter is specifically focused on these needs. What I hope for you is that you take the following steps to heart. It can make a difference and help you back to a life of security and stability and can make a way forward in life for you.

A Ray of Light for The Hurting

For many who come out of a cult, they may feel like they have nowhere to turn to, coupled with the fear of sharing and trusting someone with their complex experience. This can be a disheartening place to be and potentially create a new type of isolation. Frozen in fear of what others might think and rightfully so. For me, some of my greatest relief came when I would initiate expressing my experiences with people who had left the cult that we were a part of and expressed our experiences with one another. The beauty that came was a fellow feeling or new view that we had of the cult and our multiple experiences. It would give us a sense of reassurance when we saw that we were on the same page when we would reflect in retrospect to evaluate or discuss a newly found view of our previous cultic experiences. It gave me a sense of "I'm not alone in my past experiences and new or current views". This experience is universal for many people who are a part of a death or grieving group, al-anon, alcoholics anonymous, narcotics anonymous, divorce support groups as well as many other groups that seek to comfort one another through commonality or similar experiences. Through these programs, many people have been helped through the processes that these programs offer. They offer a lot of stability for people who are truly committed to these programs and processes.

Taking the first step on your part to seek help can be one of the most frightening things that you do. The feelings that surface from fear may overwhelm you and paralyze you with fear to reach out. I get it, unloading my over-the-top, complex, and troubled experience was not easy to do at times.

Mine was so complex that I wasn't even sure if I even saw my new and old reality with twenty-twenty vision. I often told myself I must be crazy and to share that view with someone would only lead them to think the same. Well, there are going to be some people that we share our experiences with that might struggle with being able to grasp or comprehend your experience. When you feel that this is the case, then you possess the right to set the boundary of not discussing your experience or trauma any further. You are in control. Not them.

My personal experiences with some of these organizations were helpful. When I was seventeen, I was required through a court order to attend a twelve-step program. Through this program and the twelve steps, I began to gain some ground and understanding about me as well as others and what made me as well as them tick. Although I didn't go completely dry from drugs and alcohol at that point, I feel that it was helpful to me. Ultimately, I went completely dry at the age of twenty-one. Finally, I was sick and tired of being sick and tired. From that point, my sobriety lasted for 28 years. I had been miraculously delivered from drugs and alcohol. Twenty-six years into my sobriety was the time that I departed the church cult that I was a part of. This landed me in multiple new environments: new friendships, new churches, new outreach groups, reassociating with family, and old friends, and becoming more relational with fellow employees. I found myself in multiple new environments and experiences. Within these circles of people, I also found that most of them drank. This ultimately led me to consider allowing myself to drink again on occasion. So, I began to drink again with the intent of keeping it under control. And then, I began to drink more frequently as well as drinking alone. About the same time that I began to drink, I began to become increasingly angry toward my wife as well as off the hinge anger toward God. The strength of my vocabulary toward God was unbridled and merited my mouth being washed out with soap that was laced with a little extra lye. The drinking alone coupled with my anger toward God as well as my wife served to amplify my drinking at times and would leave me with a huge gaping hole of loneliness. This may sound kind of sick but I think I liked going to this place mentally when I drank because it allowed me to feel exactly what I needed to feel about my reality. I also believe that I was drinking because of some of the same reasons that I drank when I was younger. And that was that "I didn't fit". Fortunately, my drinking did not escalate to the level of my teen years. This left planet earth in a safer standing.

After five years of this newly found drinking experience, I finally realized that it was not helping me, my marriage, or resolving my deep-seated traumatic experiences from childhood as well as being a part of a church cult for 26 years. At this point, I googled 12- step programs in my local area and found several in the area that were entitled C.R., which stands for Celebrate Recovery. Through this organization, many people have been helped with alcoholism, drug abuse, codependency issues, sexual addictions, food-related issues, and yes, spiritual abuse. The process is biblically based and merged with the twelve-step principles that were started with alcoholics anonymous. A typical meeting or service begins with worship music and prayer as well as someone either sharing their testimony/life's experience or a short message as relates to mental health or a brief study of one of the twelve steps or eight principles (see below). After this time, attendees break into their respective groups by gender. So, those who are working on sexual addictions are with a group that is focused on that and those who are working on drug and alcohol recovery are in a group together or those who have experienced some types of spiritual abuse or life's issues are paired together. Typically, there is a focus question that is given to each group to consider and then self-reflect on how it relates to them as an individual and subsequently shares how the question: relates to their life experience, how they have been impacted by their experience concerning the question posed. Also, at times there is an opportunity given to share something that is going on in your life currently or in the past. In these circles or at these times is when you may feel that someone else in the group has a fellow feeling or experience and you may find comfort for your soul or direction for your life. When we begin to own our life's issues or shoulder them with God's help and begin to open up to others about them is when we can begin the healing process. The following twelve steps have been rewritten to be more palatable or reflective for people who have experienced spiritual abuse.

12 Steps to Recovery from Spiritual Abuse:

1. We came to a place where we realized we were disillusioned and traumatized by our spiritual or religious experience in a church or cult or any other religious entity.

2. We came to a place where we asked God to help us have a clearer understanding of Him and what happened in our religious experiences.

3. We made a decision to allow God to help us discover His clear view for our lives even if we struggle to trust Him because of our spiritually destructive experiences.

4. We made a searching effort to look into

our past and make a list of destructive forces, concepts, experiences, and people that impacted our souls.

5. We shared how we felt about these destructive experiences with God and others that we trust and that have had a similar or fellow experience.

6. We asked God to help us unravel these destructive experiences and help settle us in our souls with more proper thinking or understanding.

7. In humility, we acknowledge to God where we have contributed to the spiritual abuse or harm of others in their spiritual journey.

8. We made a list of these people and where possible, made amends to them.

9. With some, we believe that direct amends could cause further issues and choose to lay them at God's feet.

A RAY OF LIGHT FOR THE HURTING

10. I had committed to taking a regular inventory of my life and how my past spiritual experiences continue to impact me.

11. Through prayer and meditation, I will continue to ask God to help me with these new discoveries so that I can be a stabilizing influence that reflects someone who has overcome and had victory.

12. I will carry my experience and message to others in need without judgment or condemnation so that they might find comfort and peace as I have.

Beginning this process is a huge step in the right direction. Although many people's religious experiences can be very complex, I would ask God to help you start to work with dismantling the simplest anomalies that you can mentally. One experience at a time. Use these as building blocks to unravel more complex and deep-seated aspects of your experience. Utilizing the above processes of expression to God and others in your new spiritual abuse or life's issues group at C.R. is where you start. It works!

To locate a local C.R. group in your area you can communicate with your state C.R. representative through the C.R. app or the C.R. website; celebraterecovery.com. Or, you can simply enter your local zip code to find the local churches in your area, via the app that offers this program. Not all locations offer or have spiritual abuse circles to participate in but they may have a group or circle that is focused on emotional abuse and or life issues. Whatever the option is that is available at your local locations, I would say it will probably be the source that begins the process to fill those empty holes in your life. I wish you well.

For further information contact:
cult.candi@gmail.com

Everyone Has a Story to Tell

At times in everyone's life, we will face obstacles and at times these obstacles can be created by our own poor choices, at times by family members, at times by people who had no idea what they were doing, and the impact that their poor choices could have on us. At times these obstacles can be God trying to grow and develop us. And yes, some will intentionally inflict harm and abuse on others. Whatever the medium that created the obstacle, we all have a choice to face and address the issue or issues that are a part of our lives. Your attitude toward these challenges can make or break your personal development and can be the equation that determines your future and or fate. When our attitude towards these obstacles or challenges of life is filled with unbridled anger and bitterness toward the offenders and the circumstantial fallout, then we will typically stagnate and become overwhelmed with hopelessness. This is why it is so important to have someone to talk to about your life's issues. If we go it alone, the healing process may, in my opinion, take longer and we may suffer longer. You may have some well-founded blame that you can lay at the feet of another. Pointing or laying the blame at another's feet is not all bad sense, it will help you in the future to be mindful of people who have similar attributes as the former perpetrator did. These bad experiences will help you to develop filters that will help you establish future boundaries for people that have harmed you or could potentially harm you and lets them know that you will not let them cross those boundaries. But, this does not and will not address the issues that may be stirring in your heart. Again, it is your story being told to the right, trusted individual or people. This is how it began with me at Celebrate Recovery. I shared my story, I shared my grief, I shared my trauma, I shared my anger, and yes, some of my deep dark secrets.

Several months before this healing process at C.R., I experienced the most over-the-top, overpowering experience of deceit and pain that had been hidden from me for fifty-three years, by 50% of my family members. And, that was that the man who I thought was my father, was not my father. To me, this was worth drinking over, and that is what I did. I medicated the pain and initially shut everyone out. Until I saw that this was God's way of healing me. He showed me one of the most painful things that a person could ever experience. And, that was that who I thought was my true father wasn't my father after all. But you say, how could revealing this be a healing point? Well, it explained the aloofness of my father in my relationship with him as I grew up. It helped me to understand that he didn't see me as his son so he didn't see much of a need to nurture me. Some examples of this are in the paragraphs that follow.

Healing alone can leave you lonely and wondering if anyone cares. Holding on to your story can also rob people of the inspiration that you offer through your horrific experience and victory. People need the ray of light that you can offer. You can give them a whole new perspective and a future hope of recovery from whatever the issue is that has traumatized them deeply.

For me, my anger toward God was deep-seated. I also expressed this to others in group sessions while attending C.R. Within a few months of expressing this at times, my great healing came. It wasn't because of anything that was expressed by others to me and it did not come about through therapy. But I believe it came when God saw that I had a heart that wanted to be healed and then He simply enlightened me. What he showed me, as expressed in the previous chapter, was that "His people are not promised nice and neatly packaged lives". I thought that God owed me a nice and neatly packaged conventional lifestyle. When I saw this, I surrendered my anger and my pride of entitlement. So, onto my short bio.

Star date 1970, at the age of three I had experienced my first taste with the man who I would come to know as my father. And, that first encounter, would pretty much set the stage for the type of relationship that we would have as I grew up. While in the garage and observing all the things that were available for a three-year-old to feast his eyes on, I discovered in the rafters a sailboat. So, I proceeded to ask my father, "why don't you use that"? He responded, "because I had you"! I felt the ouch then at three and I still can kind of feel it today. For many of you, you are saying to yourself, that boat could have been used as a relationship developer between a father and son. I agree! But somehow that was not the way it registered with the man who raised me.

Let's fast forward the clock two years to my fifth birthday. Upon opening a gift that was a book, I came up with the idea of asking my father to read it to me. What a novel idea. His response was to allow me onto his lap, read one page, possibly two or maybe even three, and then say," that is it". Meaning book time was over. I believe these types of experiences with my father set the stage to struggle with fatherly acceptance.

Now onto a couple of funnier stories. At the age of five, I entered the public school system and experienced the blessings of finger painting, candy, naps, crayons, and frogs. Yes, I said frogs! One morning while en route to school, I came up with the brilliant idea to skip school with my buddy Bradley and go frogging down at a local park. He was gamer for the experience. What five-year-old wouldn't want to go frogging? And, sure as can be, we caught more frogs that day than I could count at that point in my life. Post frogging, while en route to I'm not sure where I spotted my babysitter who was out vehemently looking for me since the school authorities alerted her that I was a no-show. Before I could jump for cover, she spotted me and immediately projected her vehicle toward me, jumped out of the car, and verbally tung lashed me. I gotta stop right here and say that the frogging adventure far outweighed the tung lashes. The final judgment and sentence; trial without a jury. I was sentenced by the principal to complete expulsion. Yes, I said "expulsion". But wait, shouldn't my sentence have been a little lighter? Yah! Like maybe taking my carpet bed away at nap time or letting all the other kids eat candy while I watch. I mean, come on now, this was just a little over the top. So, away I went to another school, another babysitter, new teachers, and a whole new environment.

So, with the new school and my inability to focus on academics, I decided to pursue my future career of becoming a permit-less builder/contractor. Yes, I was a highly skilled fort builder. I was truly a visionary when it came to structural composition and material etiquette. Shortly before lunch ended while at school, I decided to hightail it over to my buddy's house to complete the fort that we had been working on. There is just a little bit of a problem with this whole process. I left my buddy at school while I proceeded to build the fort the way I wanted to on his parent's piece of real estate. O.K., so I was a little short-sighted and inconsiderate. I should have invited him like I invited Bradley. So, onto my miscalculation and fall. During my building endeavor, my friend's mom, who was a stay-at-home mom, decided to come out and visit me. She proceeded to ask me how it was going and shouldn't I be in school? My response was," school got out early". Brilliant response! Then why wasn't her son home from school as well? I mean, we both went to the same school. O.K., so I wasn't the brightest light bulb. But even Huckleberry Finn and Tom Sawyer would have been impressed with my vision of frogging, fort building, and cutting school. Yes, the three of us lived in a parallel universe separated by about one hundred years. So, once again, I was caught and sentenced to trial without a jury. And you guessed correctly, the principal at this school expelled me as well. As a quick side note, this principal would later be the principal at my high school who would ultimately hand me my diploma as I walked across the stage way back in 1985. So, I know what you readers are thinking at this point, "there seems to be a pattern developing in his life". Yes, you are correct!

With this early life of crime of two expulsion felonies on my record by the age of six, it was certain that I was destined for a landslide of confusion academically within the public school system. Within time of being at my now third elementary school, the teacher that I then had, realized that I needed help academically. This ultimately equated to my being placed in a special needs class. This transition of academic structure and learning ultimately set the stage for me to struggle with my view of myself. I felt separated from others my age at school and felt overpowered by being viewed as stupid. Ultimately in time, I was able to overcome academically and was consistently on the dean's list during my junior high school years. Although I was able to correct my educational struggles, it did not change my view of myself.

Back to my life of crime! At age nine, while walking through the school corridor on a Saturday, I came across a couple of buddies that were throwing rocks at the school windows and shattering them. Reluctantly I joined them and went along with their admonishing me to vandalize the school room where we had thrown the rocks at. After departing this Saturday outing, I went home troubled about what I had done and went to sleep, hoping that what I had just done would go away and that I would not get caught. Well, I was able to suppress the mental distress of my crime some, but ultimately the authorities were able to capture my fingerprints and I was headed downtown for questioning. You got it, police interrogation at age nine. So, I confessed, the authorities slapped my hands, and off to my fourth and last elementary school.

After completing my fourth and final elementary school residency, I moved on to junior high and all the drama that would ensue: drug abuse, drug dealing, alcohol abuse, and sexual promiscuity just to name a few of the obvious attributes that I was developing in my life and that would soon begin to define me and my reputation at school. By the time I had finished my final year of junior high, I had developed an appetite for drugs and alcohol and had developed a complete disregard for any authority. This included my parents as well as law enforcement. I also was beginning to experience the pain of a relationship with a young lady who I liked but she had abandoned me in the relationship for another guy, who was another real winner. This was the tipping point for me mentally. This is where I flipped my middle finger at the world and began to consume rum as if I lived in the middle of a sugarcane field and there was no end to its freshly squeezed venom. By the time I was sixteen, I had become a blackout drinker and could stomach a fifth of rum myself. At this point, I was beginning the medication process of my life that I would not unwrap till decades later even though I went sober for twenty-eight years beginning from the age of twenty-one.

With this great drinking skill that I had developed, also came multiple experiences with law enforcement and consequences for my actions. My defiance of authority ultimately landed me in and out of the juvenile system. Ultimately during my senior year, I stood trial for multiple offenses: possession of a stolen vehicle, breaking in entry, drunk driving, and hit and run. I was facing (if I was an adult) four to five years in prison. My fate!? The judge sentenced me to a total of six months' time at the Sacramento County Boys Ranch. Accompanied by court order to attend a twelve-step program while incarcerated. In retrospect, I got what I deserved. I was out of control and pissed off at the world.

At this point in my life, I began to have fear of where I was, and who I had become, and was concerned about the possibility of spending my future in the prison system. I was separated from family, friends, and my day-to-day environment. Although I was mixed in with about one hundred other wards, I was in my heart, all alone. I had to look into the mirror of my life. And, that is what I did.

While attending the twelve-step program as well as participating in a bible study of my own free will, I began to see myself and my destructive conduct. I realized the multiple people I had hurt and the sin that gripped my life. I began the inventory process of my life and began to acknowledge to God who I was and cried out with brokenness to Him for forgiveness. Although I became a child of God at this point, I did not grasp the transaction that had taken place. After leaving the boy's ranch I had become very conscientious of God, day to day.

With little guidance at this point in my life and struggling to focus on a stabilizing future vision for my life's function, I continued to drink and do drugs. With this conduct carrying my life and having also become a child of God, I was conflicted. I struggled with who I was and at times would try to clean myself up and make myself acceptable to God only to repeat my same old sins. This would discourage me and I would ultimately throw in the towel, so to speak, and give up on any pursuit of God. I would condemn myself from His presence or acceptance that I so desperately needed to feel.

By the age of twenty-one, I was in a vacuum of loneliness and discouragement and was at a point in my life where I knew I needed to change. And that I did. With fervent brokenness, I cried out for deliverance from the vices that gripped my life and surrendered at Christ's feet and accepted his forgiveness into the core of my soul. From this point forward is when I began to seek God and apply the Bible to my own life. I was beginning to change little by little from within and I was fervently in the Word.

Though I had a new beginning at this point, the painful issues of how I viewed myself and the effects of my father's and mother's influence or lack of influence and my elementary school educational struggles would haunt me for years to come. Within time of this newly lived spiritual journey, I became a part of a church, as mentioned in the introduction to this book, that I thought would help me through my life's struggles as well as give my life some stability. But what it did was the exact opposite. It only served to amplify or exasperate some of my mental struggles. Typically, within a legalistic/pharisaical church structure, people will commonly struggle with feelings of inadequacy. They can also struggle with their value before God and feel like they will never measure up. So, in short, it served to amplify or exacerbate issues that were already existing in my life.

I thank God, that today, I can say because of Celebrate Recovery, some therapy, some understanding friends, and a God that heals, that I have grown in these areas and have experienced some freedom! Thank you for reading.

Epilogue

For some of you who have read this book in its entirety, you may be wondering why I did not use a lot of scripture or address multiple concepts theologically. The reason is simple. Most people who have been spiritually abused can be very closed off to scriptural or theological correctness or instruction. What they deeply want is someone who can understand them. The last thing that they should feel from anyone trying to embrace them in their religiously abusive aftermath is to feel browbeaten with the scriptures.

In America, it is reported that over 1% of the population has been connected to a cult directly or impacted indirectly by a family member who has been a part of one. In my opinion, I think the percentage is much higher. With thousands having been impacted by horrific religious or cultic trauma, that leaves a huge and gaping hole of needs for people who may have become destitute of real help and real friends who are willing to extend an arm of strength to help them through the fire and ashes. Fortunately, I had many people that crossed my path that were a source of strength and building blocks that helped stabilize me. To these people, I say thank you for your source of strength and encouragement. And also, there were some old or former cult acquaintances that I steered away from for my mental safety. I'm sure this left some of them feeling very hurt or angry but I needed to work on myself and my cultic recovery and I felt that some would inadvertently affect that process if I interacted with them. To you, I am sorry. Ultimately, it was the Creator of heaven and Earth that brought new solace to my life. If it truly was God who led me to this church cult and through it only to become more knowledgeable of the subject and to one day help others who have had similar

EPILOGUE

experiences, then I will take it, since God has given to me over and above all that I could have ever asked for. His great love for you and me is constant and the blood he shed for your soul to be redeemed is perfect to wash you white as snow. All you need to do is cry out to Him with your brokenness, believing in Him and His great name. This process will heal you day after day!

Made in the USA
Monee, IL
20 January 2023

25657063R00075